# The Green Office
## A Business Guide

# The Green Office
## A Business Guide

ALAN CALDER

**IT Governance Publishing**

Every possible effort has been made to ensure that the information contained in this book is accurate at the time of going to press, and the publishers and the author cannot accept responsibility for any errors or omissions, however caused. No responsibility for loss or damage occasioned to any person acting, or refraining from action, as a result of the material in this publication can be accepted by the publisher or the author.

Apart from any fair dealing for the purposes of research or private study, or criticism or review, as permitted under the Copyright, Designs and Patents Act 1988, this publication may only be reproduced, stored or transmitted, in any form, or by any means, with the prior permission in writing of the publisher or, in the case of reprographic reproduction, in accordance with the terms of licences issued by the Copyright Licensing Agency. Enquiries concerning reproduction outside those terms should be sent to the publishers at the following address:

IT Governance Publishing
IT Governance Limited
Unit 3, Clive Court
Bartholomew's Walk
Cambridgeshire Business Park
Ely
Cambridgeshire
CB7 4EH
United Kingdom

_www.itgovernance.co.uk_

© Alan Calder 2009
The author has asserted the rights of the author under the Copyright, Designs and Patents Act, 1988, to be identified as the author of this work.

First published in the United Kingdom in 2009
by IT Governance Publishing.

ISBN 978-1-84928-004-4

# FOREWORD

Green IT[1] will be a critical component of organisational IT and compliance strategies from 2009 onwards.

There is a range of views about what, exactly, Green IT is. At the heart of the debate[2] about the environmental role of IT, there is usually an acknowledgement that the world's information and communications technologies consume a growing amount of power and have a measurably significant carbon footprint; and that more and more people in the industrialised world today actually work in and from offices which, themselves, have a significant carbon footprint.

Regardless of one's individual position or the reality of the argument about the causes of global climate change, there are a number of aspects of modern office practice which contribute to the problem. It is equally clear that changes in these practices can have beneficial commercial impacts as well as contributing to 'saving the planet'.

As consumers become more concerned about the planetary future, green organisations are increasingly better positioned to win market share;

---

[1] Throughout this report, the term 'IT' (Information Technology) has been used rather than 'ICT' (Information and Communication Technology). The two terms are synonymous, ICT being the preferred acronym in education and government.
[2] See *The Green Agenda: A Business Guide* www.itgovernance.co.uk/products/2202 for an executive overview of the components of this debate.

an active environmental awareness is also more in tune with the expectations of today's workforce, many of whom are already accustomed in their daily life to applying the environmental mantra of *Reduce, Reuse, Recycle*.

While all organisations must be cognisant of a growing range of environmental IT regulations, what we call Green IT Compliance,[3] a green office is also a cost-effective office. The deployment of green initiatives is likely to have a directly beneficial impact on the corporate bottom line.

This guide was written specifically to help cost-conscious, environmentally-minded organisations identify practical and straightforward ways of reducing both the corporate cost base and their carbon footprint.

---

[3] See *Compliance for Green IT*, ITGP, 2009
http://www.itgovernance.co.uk/products/2199.

# ABOUT THE AUTHOR

Alan Calder is a leading author on information security and IT governance issues. He is Chief Executive of IT Governance Limited, the one-stop-shop for books, tools, training and consultancy on Governance, Risk Management and Compliance. He is also Chairman of the Board of Directors of CEME, a public-private sector skills partnership, and a non-executive director of The Outsourced Training Company, both of which are ISO14001-certified organisations.

Alan is an international authority on IT Governance and, with Steve Moir, originated the innovative Calder-Moir IT Governance framework. He is also an international expert on ISO27001 (formerly BS7799), the international security standard, about which he wrote, with colleague Steve Watkins, the definitive compliance guide, *IT Governance: A Manager's Guide to Data Security and BS7799/ISO17799.* This work is based on his experience of leading the world's first successful implementation of BS7799 and had its 4th edition published in May 2008. It is also the basis for the UK Open University's postgraduate course on information security.

Other books written by Alan include: *The Case for ISO27001; ISO27001 – Nine Steps to Success; IT Governance: Guidelines for Directors; IT Governance Today: A Practitioner's Handbook;* and *IT Regulatory Compliance in the UK.* His more recent work includes a number of Green IT titles.

## *About the author*

Alan is a frequent media commentator on information security and IT governance issues, and has contributed articles and expert comment to a wide range of trade, national and online news outlets.

Alan was previously CEO of Wide Learning, a supplier of e-learning; of Focus Central London, a training and enterprise council; and of Business Link London City Partners, a government agency focused on helping growing businesses to develop. He was a member of the Information Age Competitiveness Working Group of the UK Government's Department for Trade & Industry and was, until recently, a member of the DNV Certification Services Certification Committee, which certifies compliance with international standards including ISO27001 and ISO14001, the environmental management system standard.

# ACKNOWLEDGEMENTS

Much of the original content of this pocket guide is drawn from the IT Governance Best Practice Report on the subject of Green IT, which was developed by our in-house research and analysis team and published toward the end of 2008. *Green IT – Reality, Benefits & Best Practices*[4] provides comprehensive, current guidance for organisations addressing the challenge of greening their IT operations. This pocket guide, on the other hand, is designed for company directors and executives as a specific guide to the growing range of regulatory requirements that, driven by the green agenda, are impacting businesses and IT organisations everywhere.

---

[4] Read about, and purchase, this report from http://www.itgovernance.co.uk/products/1933.

# CONTENTS

# INTRODUCTION

The majority in today's industrialised economies are knowledge workers rather than manual workers. They work primarily in offices and rely on Information and Communications Technology infrastructures to support their daily activity.

Any organisation pursuing an environmentally friendly strategy – whether it is a focused Green IT strategy or a broader corporate strategy to reduce carbon footprint and increase environmental effectiveness – will obviously take account of the carbon footprint of their offices and all the activity that goes on inside them. Key areas for consideration must include:

- energy usage and power consumption (for powering the ICT infrastructure as well as for heating and lighting) in the office
- growing data storage requirements, which increase the carbon footprint of the office
- the computing infrastructure that supports office workers
- paper usage – always a significant aspect of the office's carbon footprint
- office supplies
- printing, printer inks and toners
- the potential for recycling (with its attendant security issues)
- cleaning and janitorial activities
- office furniture
- staff refreshments and catering services
- travel costs.

## Introduction

Of course, any office today must comply with a growing range of environmental regulation; it is not the purpose of this guide to advise on those issues, but the guide does introduce ISO14001, the environmental management system standard, which provides a blueprint for organisations which are seeking a more systematic approach to how they deploy, implement and manage a more environmentally aware corporate policy.

# CHAPTER 1: YOUR CARBON FOOTPRINT

The starting point for a Green Office strategy is usually a measurement of the organisation's current carbon footprint. Once this has been calculated, plans for reduction can be prioritised and progress measured.

The carbon footprint shows the environmental impact of an organisation by measuring its output of what are considered to be the main climate change (or greenhouse) gases. Carbon footprint, therefore, relates to the amount of greenhouse gases produced by the organisation every day as a result of burning fossil fuels for electricity, heating, transportation and so on. For this reason, carbon footprint calculations are also often known as $CO_2$ calculations. Carbon footprint is expressed in units of tonnes (or kg) of carbon dioxide ($CO_2$) equivalent.

Carbon footprint calculation is not yet an exact science. The most widely applied method is the GHG (GreenHouseGas) protocol[5].

- The primary footprint measures the organisation's direct (controllable) emissions of $CO_2$ from the burning of fossil fuels on site (in factory operations, for instance), and from the transportation of goods produced (e.g. by car or plane). Organisations which own or control the sources of primary emissions can therefore take direct action to reduce their

---

[5] http://www.ghgprotocol.org.

primary footprint; many office-based organisations do not have a primary footprint.

- The secondary footprint measures the indirect $CO_2$ emissions from the whole lifecycle of products used in the business, including their manufacture, delivery and eventual breakdown. This secondary footprint includes power consumption for running ICT. The only real control the organisation has over this aspect of its carbon footprint is in terms of what it purchases and how it controls consumption.

- The tertiary footprint measures the $CO_2$ emissions of outsourced suppliers with which the company has contracts, and those from employee commuting.

Calculating a primary carbon footprint is a time-consuming and detailed task. It requires the identification of all items which consume electricity, and the creation of estimates for how much power each item consumes in the average working day. The item's carbon footprint is then calculated from standard tables of the average $CO_2$ produced in order to provide a given level of power. For instance, an average PC workstation (less than three years old, with an LCD screen) will use 0.6kW per hour of the day. This produces 0.527 kg of $CO_2$. Across a working year, this equates to 1,209.6 kWh and 637.45 kg (0.637 tonnes) of $CO_2$.

Many carbon calculation applications are available, as a quick Internet search will demonstrate. Most, however, are specifically designed for consumer use, dealing with carbon emissions caused by shopping, car journeys, flights and so on. There are also carbon calculators available to measure the overall carbon footprint of buildings. The GHG Protocol Initiative Foundation provides a range of free tools, including a calculator for the service sector, which are probably the most thorough ones currently available.[6] They come with detailed guidance on how to do the calculations.

There is also the GHG Protocol Corporate Standard, which provides guidance for companies and other organisations preparing a GHG emissions inventory. It deals with the accounting and reporting of the six greenhouse gases covered by the Kyoto Protocol: carbon dioxide ($CO_2$), methane ($CH_4$), nitrous oxide ($N_2O$), hydrofluorocarbons (HFCs), perfluorocarbons (PFCs), and sulphur hexafluoride ($SF_6$). It was designed to help companies prepare a GHG inventory that would be a true and fair account of their emissions, through the use of standardised approaches and principles.

None of the existing calculators are specifically designed for the IT organisation seeking a handle on its own activity. The *Green IT CO2 Calculator*[7] is an IT-orientated tool that helps organisations assess their IT carbon footprint.

Organisations wanting a more precise, customised calculation can arrange for a consultancy firm

---

[6] http://www.ghgprotocol.org/calculation-tools/service-sector.
[7] Available free from:
http://www.itgovernance.co.uk/green-it.aspx.

to come and perform a detailed survey and calculation.

## Calculate your carbon footprint

Whatever tool you choose, the first step in any Green Office strategy is to calculate the carbon footprint of the office. It is worth spending a short period refining your calculation so that you can reuse it to monitor progress on a regular basis.

For most organisations, the focus will mostly be on secondary and tertiary footprints, which will require consideration of the activities below.

### *Primary footprint*

- Stationary fuel-burning units on site (e.g. gas- or oil-fired heating systems – your data will come from records of raw fuel purchases).
- Employee commuting or business travel in company-owned cars or planes. You may need to create or redesign existing reports in order to capture this data.

### *Secondary footprint:*

- Data centres.[8]
- Numbers of workstations, thin clients, laptops, tower computers, free-standing computer screens (CRT or LCD), and printers, copiers,

---

[8] This pocket guide does not deal with data centres; see *The Governance of Green IT* (www.itgovernance.co.uk/products/2106) and *The Green Data Center*, both by George Spafford, published by ITGP.

faxes and MFDs (multi-function devices) – all this information gathered through an inventory and logically tied in to any CMDB (configuration management database).

- Amount and type of paper consumed (procurement records).

- Type of office supplies, furniture and staff refreshments (procurement records).

- Power purchased for heating, cooling, lighting, office machinery and other appliances (utility bills).

### *Tertiary footprint*

- Employee commuting (you may need to create questionnaires to discover the various ways that employees commute).
- Carbon footprint of outsourced third-party suppliers, e.g. contracted IT service organisations, payroll bureaux and so on. You will need to ask them for this information and, in many instances, you will find that they do not have it. This should not derail your overall Green IT project, although it might, in the long term, affect who you purchase those services from.

### Create a prioritised action plan

Once you have calculated the carbon footprint of your office(s), you can set about the creation of a prioritised action plan to reduce their carbon footprint. Focus first on those areas where you can achieve the most direct reductions and, simultaneously, the most measurable financial bottom-line impact. The chapters that follow deal with how savings can be achieved in each of the identified areas.

# CHAPTER 2: REDUCING YOUR DIRECT CARBON COST

For most organisations, reducing the primary carbon footprint of their offices will consist in two actions:

1   reducing the amount of fuel consumed in onsite gas- or oil-fired boilers, through plant efficiency and/or controlled usage
2   reducing the number of business miles commuted by management and members of staff in cars and planes owned (or controlled) by the organisation.

## Onsite boilers

Boilers that are installed in smaller offices are usually of the domestic variety and their default settings are, therefore, those appropriate to a domestic setting: they come on in the morning and later in the afternoon, then continue burning until bedtime. Whatever time that may be, it is certainly long after most staff have left the office. Similarly, the default setting for domestic boilers is to be on through most of the weekend, which is exactly when most staff are not in the office.

The first simple step is, therefore, to ensure that all boilers installed anywhere on corporate facilities are modern boilers, with timing mechanisms that enable them to be set so that both heating and hot water are available at times appropriate for the office. It also makes sense to ensure that all boilers have thermostats and that the thermostatic setting ensures that the boiler does not continue burning once the room is at the required temperature. For reference, in the UK there is a legal minimum indoor temperature, which is 13°C (55°F) for those doing strenuous work, and 16°C (61°F) for those behind a desk. Many staff may prefer warmer conditions than this, but you are also entitled to suggest that they wear warmer clothes! The optimum office temperature is typically 19°C to 21°C and, as a 1°C reduction in room temperature can save 6–8% on heating costs and $CO_2$ emissions, it is certainly worth exploring exactly how low room temperatures can realistically go.

It should be noted that, while there is a legal minimum temperature, there is no legal maximum temperature. Although it is obvious that central heating systems should be switched off once the cold period has passed, there is no legal requirement to install or operate air conditioning systems. The *Workplace Regulations* (1992) do stipulate that, during working hours, the temperature in all workplaces inside buildings must be 'reasonable', but 'reasonable' is not defined.

There are, of course, good reasons – measured in terms both of morale and employee health – for ensuring that employees are neither too hot nor too cold in the workplace. Sensible organisations will ensure that significant changes to heating arrangements will be discussed with staff, and their support and buy-in encouraged.

There are a number of basic rules which it is advisable to advertise to staff or users throughout the office, and whose benefit will be felt in both the primary and secondary carbon footprint reduction:

- close doors and windows when heating and air conditioning is on
- report/repair doors and windows that do not seal correctly
- ensure that radiators are not blocked by furniture
- dress appropriately for the weather conditions – wear layers in winter and cooler clothing in summer
- avoid the use of portable electric heaters, as these usually have a more significant carbon footprint than the heating system
- ensure that heating and cooling systems are not running at the same time
- remember that natural ventilation uses about half as much energy as air conditioning
- report/repair faults and malfunctions in heating and cooling systems, and ensure that they are all serviced to schedule.

Larger organisations will find it advisable to survey how all their offices and buildings are heated. Have HVAC engineers assess the heating equipment to ensure that it is working to optimum efficiency and that appropriate building insulation and effective heating ducting is in place. Make sure that radiators have individual controls so that they can, when necessary, be turned off individually. Examine technologies and approaches for ensuring that unoccupied buildings and rooms are neither heated nor cooled. Ensure that the entire heating, cooling and ventilation system is serviced regularly and kept working efficiently. Ensure that air and fuel filters are replaced regularly.

## Corporate transportation

Calculate the carbon footprint of all transportation assets owned by the company and compare it with the likely carbon footprint from forcing executives to use commercial flights, and employees to use public transport or their own motor cars, both for business travel and personal commuting.

In many cases, the carbon footprint reduction – and the corporate bottom line benefits – make such a policy change worth debating! Otherwise, many of the guidelines which are discussed later in the chapter on transportation apply to company-owned assets as well.

# CHAPTER 3: ENERGY EFFICIENCY IN THE OFFICE

Gary Hird, IT Strategy Manager at UK retailer, John Lewis, says an awareness of energy efficiency fits with the company's ethos which emphasises responsible capitalism and employee democracy. 'I joined the company in 1989,' he says, 'and one of the first things I noticed was that every light switch had a sticker next to it, reading "Switch off, you're burning my bonus". It made pure sense to do that because we all benefited as a result.'[9]

The obvious starting point for any energy efficiency planning is to ensure that the organisation's energy purchasing is as cost-effective as possible. Utility companies all over the world do compete with one another, and organisations should initiate the power-reduction component of their Green Office project by thoroughly reviewing the price packages available to them from all interested suppliers. Better deals are sometimes available for dual supply (i.e. both electricity and gas) contracts.

Alternative energy sources – from solar panels to wind turbines – are beyond the scope of this book; investment in such alternative power sources will not necessarily generate a return on investment matching that available through following the straightforward guidance here.

---

[9] *Managing the Company's Carbon Footprint: The Emerging Role of ICT*, Economist Intelligence Unit, 2008.

The previous chapter dealt with heating and cooling in the office. The guidance that applies to ensuring that gas- and oil-fired heating systems are effective also applies to any electric heating systems. Electric fan heaters are expensive to operate; storage heaters and electric oil-filled heaters can be used effectively to spot-heat specific rooms or other environments.

The modern office is packed with electronic equipment that is left switched on most of the day and, in many cases, overnight as well. While actual power consumption will vary from office to office, IT and electronic office equipment will, on average, take between 9% and 15% of the organisation's total power consumption, with desktop PCs and their monitors usually responsible for the largest part of that. A desktop computer, used eight hours a day, generates over 600 kilograms of harmful greenhouse gases each year.

Significant energy savings (these will be in the secondary carbon footprint) come from aggressive application of power-saving capabilities in all office equipment. In many cases, power-saving modes can be configured and either controlled centrally or built in to the standard desktop image. Experiment with aggressive settings for automatic sleep mode; scale back from the level at which most people complain to the one at which only a few are discommoded but most can cope.

## Reducing office energy requirements

Tips for Green Office energy reductions include those below.[10]

- Configure monitors to turn off after 5–20 minutes of inactivity. Monitors should also have a password-protected screensaver that comes on whenever the computer is unattended.

- Configure the hard drives on workstations and laptops to turn off after 20–30 minutes of inactivity.

- Get desktop computers or laptops to go into standby or sleep mode after 30–70 minutes of inactivity.

- Ensure that all office equipment is switched off after hours; staff may need to be (re)trained to power down their workstations before they leave; a member of staff should check each area to make sure this has been done.

- Shared office equipment should also be powered down; there may be some appliances (such as fax machines) that need to be kept on overnight, but most printers, copiers, and so on do not.

- There may be some appliances whose continued uptime is considered essential; each of these cases should be considered on its merits and an appropriate decision made and carried out. The fact that some appliances may

---

[10] Tips for Energy Smart offices, Energy Smart Australia, www.deus.nsw.gov.au/energy/information%20for%20co nsumers/working%20energy%20smart/Tips%20for%20 Energy%20Smart%20offices.asp.

need to stay up should not be allowed to justify keeping all of them up!

- Ensure your computer, photocopier, printer and fax machine have the ENERGY STAR[8] power management feature enabled.

- Plan to do critical upgrades and virus patch rollouts during quiet patches in the day (e.g. lunchtime) rather than requiring all the computers to be left on overnight so that, from time to time, automated updates can be applied. Alternatively, deploy software that will ensure that patches and upgrades are applied at boot up or at close down.

- Purchase smart plug strips[11] for devices such as printers, monitors, calculators, or typewriters that do not need to have power reach them unless they are being used. These plug strips cost £5–10 each and they can each reduce the carbon output of your organisation by up to 131.5 kilograms per year.

- Portable computers use less energy than desktop models, and ink jet printers generally use far less energy per page than laser models.

ENERGY STAR also provides advice[12] on selecting the most appropriate software (and there are both freeware and commercial software solutions available) to save electricity

---

[11] mydeco.com/product/intellipanel-energy-saving-8-way-plug-strip-for-desktops/7e59a29dfefde72a6e4322d522e142e8e09b8e9b/.

[12] http://www.energystar.gov/index.cfm?c=power_mgt.pr_power_management.

and reduce costs by implementing different power/sleep modes.

## Lighting

Effective reductions in power used in office lighting depend on a combination of changes to light bulbs and lighting systems, and the re-education and training of users. Management should take a lead in ensuring that energy efficiency is sought in terms of lighting.

- Use motion-detecting light switches and set them to turn lighting off whenever rooms are unoccupied.
- Use compact fluorescent light (CFL)[13] bulbs wherever possible; these have significantly reduced power requirements and, when combined with an ENERGY STAR light fitting, can be particularly effective.
- Don't leave lights on in unoccupied areas
  - o last one out at the end of the day should always switch off the lights
  - o last one out of a meeting room should switch off the lights.
- Switch off lights that are not needed
  - o these could be in offices, corridors, meeting rooms, toilets and kitchen areas, and so on
  - o don't switch on all lights when only a few are needed

---

[13] www.greenpeace.org.uk/climate/cfl-bulbs-the-myths.

o use local desk lights if only a few people are in the building/office.

- Always make maximum use of daylight. Natural daylight is better to work in as well as carbon and cost free. If staff get an uncomfortable glare on their computer screen, look at rearranging the desk-top before closing blinds and turning on the lights. Remember that sitting near a window could enable someone to see confidential information, so this aspect must also be considered.
- Reduce decorative lighting wherever possible.
- Report/repair faulty lighting promptly

  o a flickering tube uses more electricity, as well as being very distracting.

## Reconfiguring the office

The advice above is useful in terms of reducing the energy usage in the average office without disrupting the office network. More significant savings become available as organisations focus on reconfiguring enterprise networks to maximise their efficiency.

- Deploy ENERGY STAR[14] 4.0 compliant workstations, printers, faxes and other electronic equipment. These use 15–25% less energy than standard computers, and

---

[14] ENERGY STAR ratings were first created by the US EPA in 1992 and have since been adopted in Australia, Canada, Japan, New Zealand, Taiwan and the European Union. The EU also has an alternative certification, the TCO: http://en.wikipedia.org/wiki/TCO_Certification.

are shipped with power management features enabled.

- Reconfigure the office network to reduce the number of printers that are available for use – particularly energy-intensive high-volume laser printers. It may, of course, be necessary to ensure that the time and motion impact of such changes do not reduce overall office efficiency.

- Reconfigure the office network to reduce the number of copiers and fax machines; a number of individual machines could be replaced with a radically smaller number of MFDs (Multifunction Devices, or All-In-Ones, that combine printer, fax and copier in a single unit).

- While redesigning the network, it would be worth examining the extent to which an overhaul of the various business processes could lead to a streamlining and consequent reduction in appliance requirements. One possible approach might be to reduce the amount of paper in use in the office, by shifting very substantially to digital record keeping (as discussed later in this guide) combined with digital fax/electronic mailbox integration to reduce the requirements for fax machines and paper.

- A reconfigured network could also be extensively based on thin clients and cloud computing, which are both discussed later in this guide.

# CHAPTER 4: DATA STORAGE

E-mail has become the standard means for individuals and organisations to communicate with one another and amongst themselves. The proliferation of free Internet e-mail accounts allowing substantial e-mail attachments, and the digitisation of books, pictures, music, video and films, all contribute to a significant increase in processing and storage capacity requirements.

E-mails and e-mail attachments can very rapidly and exponentially increase server storage requirements. For example, if one person sends a 1MB PowerPoint™ presentation to 10 colleagues and they each move that e-mail into their own PST file, there will be 10MB of duplicated data.

The PST file is a type of file which is used by Microsoft Outlook to store e-mail messages, calendar items and other Outlook data for an individual user. The PST file can be held on the server or on a shared company network, or locally on the user's hard drive.

If the PST files for each of the 10 recipients of the original e-mail are then backed up on a 10-day cycle, the original 1MB PowerPoint presentation will now require 100 MB of back-up storage.

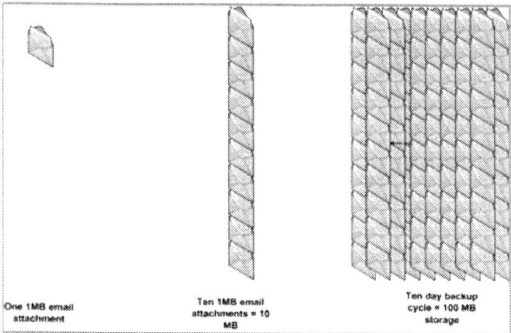

**Figure 1: The exponential growth of e-mail attachments stored in the server**
Derived from *Death to PST files: The Hidden Costs of E-mail*, Messagelabs, 2008

Data deduplication (also referred to as 'intelligent compression' or 'single-instance storage') is a process used to identify and delete multiple instances of the same item of data. This can refer to data held in databases as well as e-mail. E-mail deduplication can be carried out manually (by requiring users, for instance, to delete all copies of e-mails that they hold, or stripping attachments off e-mails) but this is a time-consuming, unproductive task that also risks the deletion of critical data.

Duplicate data in databases, such as duplicate customer records or duplicate addresses can be identified and subsequently deleted using tools such as Structured Query Language (SQL) or other deduplication software.

'Single instance e-mail' is the technology that stores only one instance of an e-mail and simply places short cuts in the inboxes of addressees. This has the immediate benefit of eliminating multiple copies of any e-mail.

An example of single-instance e-mail technology is 'Enterprise Archive Solution' (EAS) provided by Autonomy Zantaz. When a message is archived with EAS, it is removed from the Exchange Server or PST file and saved in a central storage area. Every file which is saved in that area is compressed for additional storage efficiency. An algorithm is applied to ensure that only a single instance or copy of each message is saved.

The key green benefit of data deduplication and single instance e-mail storage is the reduction in data storage requirements which, in turn, reduces the energy required in the data centre and also prolongs the life of the server. This also reduces the amount of data needing to be backed up[15] off site, and can decrease the amount of backup storage required by 90%. In other words, the business benefits from data deduplication start with increasing overall data integrity, and end with reducing overall data protection costs. There are a number of software vendors that provide this technology.

The prioritisation of tackling deduplication will depend on the role of data storage in the organisation's overall carbon footprint; for many organisations, managing data storage intelligently

---

[15] *Data deduplication*, SearchStorage.com, http://searchstorage.techtarget.com/sDefinition/0,,sid5_g ci1248105,00.html.

is an activity with valuable long-term benefits in the costs of both primary data storage and backup.

Of the three available approaches (manual deduplication, automated deduplication and single instance e-mail storage) the third is the most appropriate as it best recognises the fact that e-mails are a legal corporate record and that any wilful destruction of corporate records is dangerous to an organisation's commercial activities and, possibly, illegal.

# CHAPTER 5: THIN CLIENTS

A 'thin client'[16] describes the client in a client-server system architecture in which the client depends largely on the server (or, using the Software as a Service – SaaS – model, on servers available in the 'Cloud') for processing activities. PCs, also known as work stations, do a substantial part of their processing locally on their own systems, using the comprehensive and complex software packages available from Microsoft[R], Apple[R] and others.

There is an argument that most users do not need to access most of the capability available on their PCs most of the time. Indeed, they often do not need all the formatting and other capabilities of, for instance, MS Word, if all they need to do is create a simple memo or send an e-mail.

The use of thin clients rather than PCs eliminates local workstations and centralises all applications on central or Cloud computers. Users draw down the applications they need, when they need them. As a result, organisations can save costs by reducing their power requirements across the corporate PC network, they can improve data security and, into the bargain, they can increase the lifetime of IT equipment. There are a number of significant data security benefits to a thin-client solution, including central control over application installation (no unauthorised applications can be installed), 100% first-time patching (as all

---

[16] For more on the history and status of thin client computing, see: http://en.wikipedia.org/wiki/Thin_client.

patching is done centrally), and complete control over data movement.

There are a number of vendors of thin-client software, which can be installed on PCs as well as on thin-client hardware. Indeed, solutions are available that enable a user's PC environment (including fully functioning applications) to be made available as a thin client, so that the user can access his/her desktop from any terminal.

Forrester Research[17] claims that using thin clients can reduce $CO_2$ emissions by 23%, from 237,930 kg of annual emissions for PCs, to 183,408 kg for thin clients. Forrester reports other potential green benefits, including lower power consumption, reduced noise and weight, cleaner production and downstream disposal and increased lifetime of the client hardware (5–10+ years).

Critics of the thin client alternative have not specifically rejected the identified benefits of thin clients. They have, however, argued against them on the basis of business effectiveness and user autonomy, saying that the deployment of thin clients removes autonomy and independence from users and that, in some cases, the use of thin clients would be a step backwards. Individual organisations will need to assess the potential ramifications for their organisation when considering the use of thin clients.

---

[17] *Using IT to Support Corporate Sustainability*, Euan Davis, Principal Analyst, Forrester Research, Inc., 7 May 2008.

# CHAPTER 6: PAPER

The production and use of paper is said to have a significant carbon footprint, with the additional negative impact that cutting down forests to create paper removes one of the earth's means of converting $CO_2$ back to oxygen.

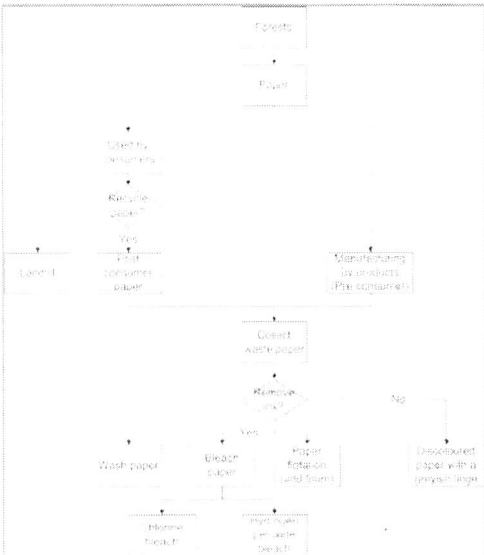

**Figure 1: Flowchart of the process used to make recycled paper**

## 6: Paper

The idea that larger users of paper (a major output of office activity) should switch to recycled paper in order to protect the earth's forests is, therefore, not surprising. Recycling, however, is a complex area and it is not always clear what the most appropriate approach to this issue might be.

The flowchart above provides a diagrammatic representation of the process used to make recycled paper, and sets the scene for a comparison of the arguments for and against recycling. There is no single, conclusive position on this issue; every organisation has to reach its own decision on the balance of benefits.

One strongly argued approach is that the best, and most efficient, thing to do with paper is to burn it for energy, rather than recycle it.[18] The argument is that paper is an organic compound that contains stored energy and can be burned for power in coal-fired plants, rather than coal. Paper burns much more cleanly than coal, and can reduce the environmental impact of polluting coal plants.

The arguments for and against recycled paper are summarised below.

**Cost**

**For** – Recycled paper has an equivalent cost to virgin paper.

**Against** – Recycled paper costs more than virgin paper.

---

[18] *The Myths of Recycling*, 9 August 2007, http://btau.newsvine.com/_news/2007/08/09/888171-the-myths-of-recycling.

6: *Paper*

## Sustainable forests

**For** – Trees help take carbon dioxide out of the atmosphere. Recycling paper reduces the number of trees which need to be felled. Paper recycling optimises the use of a valuable material and reduces the amount of virgin pulp required. Although forests are increasingly managed in a sustainable way there is a need to reduce wastage by using more recycled content. Nearly 80% of the world's original old growth forests have been logged or severely degraded.[19]

**Against** – Paper is produced from tree farms, which are subject to tight environmental regulation and reforesting. The tree forests from which paper is produced have a net positive effect on the environment.[20] Reducing the amount of paper produced would lessen this net positive effect on the environment.


## Use of chlorine

**For** – Increasingly, bleaching is carried out using chlorine-free processes. The Co-operative Financial Services Sustainability Report 2003[21] suggests that 'all paper (whether recycled or virgin fibres) should be produced using a totally chlorine-free (TCF) bleaching process in order to minimise the amount of harmful organochlorines and related dioxins that may enter the environment. This

---

[19] *Recycled Printing and Paper – The Facts*, www.alocalprinter.com/uk/recycled-paper/.
[20] *The Myths of Recycling*, q.v.
[21] CFS Paper Guidelines, www.cfs.co.uk/sustainability2003/additional/paper.htm.

means that the manufacturing process should not include the use of chlorine gas or chlorine dioxide as bleaching agents'.

**Against** – The chlorine used to bleach recycled paper releases noxious chemicals into the environment.

## Landfills

**For** – Reduce landfill – using recycled paper diverts waste paper from entering landfills. Landfills are a source of methane emissions, which are a contributor to global warming. What is equally important is that landfills are rapidly becoming full, and fewer new sites are available.[22]

**Against** – The Newswire argues that 'modern landfills are efficient, clean and generally environmentally friendly. In addition, they are often subject to tight local, state and federal regulation. The economic and environmental costs of recycling however are often muddled, and riddled with qualifications. The original landfill scare came about in the 1970s, and 1980s, as some North-eastern cities struggled to find cheap land. This situation is no longer true'.[23]

## Use of fossil fuels

**For** – No arguments.

---

[22] *Recycled Printing and Paper – The Facts*, q.v.
[23] *The Myths of Recycling*, q.v.

**Against** – The process used to convert post-recycled paper into new recycled paper involves the consumption of fossil fuels. Trees can be reforested and replanted, whereas the fossil fuels used in order to recycle cannot. When paper is initially produced out of new trees, much of the energy comes from wood by-products, rather than fossil fuels.

There are a number of important considerations for organisations that decide to use recycled paper.

The Co-operative Financial Services (CFS)[24] recommendations for ecologically-sound paper (in order of preference) are:

- 100% totally chlorine-free (TCF) and 100% post-consumer waste (pcw) recycled
- 100% TCF and 50% plus pcw recycled (with any remaining virgin fibre Forestry Stewardship Council (FSC) certified and 100% TCF)
- 100% TCF and 100% FSC certified. As above, any virgin fibres should carry the FSC logo.

They also suggest that consideration should be given to the lowest weight paper that meets the requirements of the task, such as 120 gsm for a magazine, 80–100 gsm for a letter and 60–80 gsm for a leaflet. A weight reduction reduces the total amount of paper used, and may also reduce freight and postal charges.

---

[24] CFS Paper Guidelines, q.v.

The Forest Stewardship Council (FSC)[25] is an international non-profit organisation, founded in 1993 to support the world's forests.

**Figure 2: The FSC logo**

The FSC provides standard setting, trademark assurance and accreditation services. Products carrying the FSC logo are independently certified to guarantee users and purchasers of those products that they 'meet the social, economic and ecological needs of present and future generations'.[26]

Pulpwatch[27] is an organisation which rates pulp and paper mills on their performance. Mills are rated on their performance with regard to endangered forests, bleaching, sustainable certification and social issues. Users can browse mills with an interactive map or search by mill, products or company.

---

[25] www.fsc.org.
[26] *About the Forest Stewardship Council* www.fsc.org/about-fsc.html.
[27] www.pulpwatch.org.

## Confidential waste

'Confidential waste' refers to confidential paper records that have reached their retention end date and which need to be shredded and disposed of. There is no formal guidance nor are there any regulations in the UK regarding confidential waste. Virtually anyone could set up in business claiming to dispose of confidential waste, so every client needs to carry out an appropriate level of due diligence before selecting a supplier, and to select and deploy appropriate controls (such as those recommended in ISO/IEC 27002) as part of a structured due diligence checklist and contract management approach.

The following table lists the relevant controls recommended by ISO27002. These provide a source of best practice guidance.

| A.6.2.1 | Identification of risks related to third parties |
|---------|--------------------------------------------------|
| A.6.2.3 | Addressing information security in third-party agreements |
| A.9.1.6 | Public access, delivery and loading areas |
| A.9.2.7 | Removal of property |
| A.10.2 | Monitoring and review of third-party services |

| A.10.7.2 | Disposal of media |
| A.10.8.3 | Physical media in transit |

**Table 1: The relevant controls recommended by ISO27001**
The control reference is to the Annex A designation for that control

# CHAPTER 7: REDUCE TRAVEL COSTS

Travel and commuting costs, using employees' own vehicles, public transport or commercial airlines, all form part of an organisation's tertiary carbon footprint.

It is difficult to correctly estimate the $CO_2$ emissions caused by staff commutes. The starting point is that each gallon of petrol burned releases approximately 18 kg of $CO_2$ into the air; this figure will be worse if the car is running on underinflated tyres, has roof racks and other fittings that reduce fuel efficiency, or is driven quickly or abruptly. Larger, less fuel-efficient vehicles will obviously get fewer miles per gallon of fuel and will have a worse environmental impact than smaller cars.

As a rule of thumb, a 5-mile commute (i.e. a 10-mile round trip) in an average-sized motor car will produce about 5 kg of $CO_2$ (about 0.5 kg is produced for each average mile driven). So, in a single year (220 working days) of commuting, the average commuter will produce 1,100 kg of $CO_2$. It is, therefore, worth looking at ways of reducing this environmental impact.

## Alternative commuting options

There is a plethora of alternative methods for employees to commute to work. These range from using public transport, to cycling and car pooling.

While effective car pooling[28] may require the organisation to take steps to initiate and support the activity (with intranet links, financial incentives, administrative support, and so on), it is more complex to enable employees to cycle to work in any numbers. For cycling to be an effective alternative, the employer will certainly have to provide secure storage facilities as well as changing rooms and, potentially, showers and related facilities to enable employees to be appropriately dressed in the work place. The cost-benefit analysis should take into account the fact that the provision of employee car parking costs about £1,000 per year; replacing this with support for cycling might pay off quickly.

Cycling to work has long been a preferred option for many, so much information[29] already exists to help organisations plan and implement a cycle to work policy.

## Teleworking or home working

Teleworking, the practice of employees working from home whilst being connected to their office electronically, primarily through e-mail and web services, is a logical way of reducing commuting.

The growing use of Web 2.0 technologies, such as webmail and document sharing over the Internet,

---

[28] There is a good introduction to the details of car pooling, with links to further sources of information at: http://en.wikipedia.org/wiki/Carpool.
[29] The most comprehensive guidance is from the UK Department for Transport: http://www.dft.gov.uk/pgr/roads/tpm/tal/cyclefacilities/c yclingtowork.

combined with the increased penetration of broadband mean that teleworking is now easier than ever.

The number of households and companies that have access to broadband Internet access has increased dramatically (but not consistently) around the world over the past five years.

Commuting times in Europe are greater than those in the US, with the United Kingdom having the worst commute in the European Union. British commuters have the longest journeys to work, with the average trip from home to work taking 45 minutes.[30]

However, despite this all this, it seems that it is more common for employees to spend only the occasional day working from home, rather than for teleworking to be a regular occurrence. It would seem that home working is often awarded by managers as an informal perk for high-achieving workers. Some organisations charge their employees to access e-mail from home. In 2008, the Economist Intelligence Unit conducted a survey of 345 senior executives in order to gain a deeper understanding of how companies perceive and use IT in order to save costs and reduce energy. They found that home working is not widely adopted. They reported[31] that '59% of the survey panel said that no one, or almost no one, at

---

[30] *Eco Executive*, Issue One:
http://publishing.yudu.com/Aafvk/EcoExecutiveIss1/resources/87.htm.
[31] *Managing the company's Carbon Footprint: The Emerging Role of ICT*, Economist Intelligence Unit, 2008.

their organisations works from home on a regular basis. Likewise, two-thirds (67%) of respondents said no one, or almost no one, in their organisation is given financial or material assistance to set up an office from home'.

Some companies are offering more environmentally-friendly alternatives to driving to work. Microsoft, for instance, provides shuttle buses, which are equipped with Wi-Fi so passengers can access their e-mail and Internet en route to the office.

Home working can significantly reduce an organisation's carbon footprint. Benefits include those below. [32]

- Reduced costs to the organisation in office space, heating, lighting and operating costs.
- Reduced costs to employees in travel costs.
- An organisation can include the saving in $CO_2$ emissions resulting from the employee's homeworking as a metric to support ISO14001 certification. A spokesman for BSI said 'The target for homeworking is for people who are working full time from home. For example, homeworking could be used to support certification for an organisation such as the British Standards Institute (BSI), where about half of the 2,000 employees work from home full time. However, homeworking might not be taken into account for an organisation

---

[32] *Eco Executive*, Issue One, http://publishing.yudu.com/Aafvk/EcoExecutiveIss1/resources/87.htm.

employing 10 staff, one of whom works from home once a week'.

It should be borne in mind that, whilst 'homeworking' is often touted as a panacea for reducing energy costs, it does not work for everyone. Technology is not the only consideration.

Some employees do not find it easy to maintain the self-discipline required to work from home. Other employees find it difficult working on their own all day and miss the physical presence of other employees. The culture of some organisations may just not be conducive to home working. In addition, some managers find it easier than others to be flexible and relaxed about their staff working from home. Other managers may feel that they need their staff to be physically present in the office.

In addition, whilst employers save money on operating costs, employees incur some additional costs in heating, lighting and powering their computer.

All these factors need to be taken into consideration if regular homeworking is to be a viable option.

*Virtual meetings*

A substantial part of any organisation's carbon footprint is the travel that is necessary to attend meetings – customer meetings, supplier meetings, staff meetings and so on. Virtual meetings use technology to enable employees to participate in a meeting without having to travel, and the deployment of this sort of technology can also create substantial cost savings.

The technologies that enable virtual meetings include web conferencing and collaboration tools.

## Video and web conferencing

David Coleman[33] describes the trend for the convergence of audio, video and Web (data) conferencing. In the 1990s, audio conferencing and video conferencing were available as separate software systems. They were not hugely successful, for a multitude of reasons, including expense, complexity and poor communication quality. Teleconferencing has become reasonably well-established as a means for short, voice-only meetings. More recently, though, technologies have become available which provide a combination of the three, together with additional features such as instant messaging. Web conferencing tools make it possible for organisations to deliver interactive web-based training to a global audience, as well as to work collaboratively on software and presentations. They also provide desktop sharing, whereby an application on one participant's computer can be shared with many other/remote participants.

Examples of Web conferencing tools include WebEx, GoToMeeting[R] and Microsoft[R] Live Meeting. Webex also provides instant messaging.

Video conferencing has also improved significantly during this century, and applications

---

[33] *Collaboration 2.0*, David Coleman and Stewart Levine, Happy About, 2008.

are now available to help organisations stage meetings that can effectively handle many-to-many video conference communications.

## Collaboration tools

Collaboration tools use functions designed to aid internal collaboration and communication within organisations. This includes creating and sharing team documents, creating individual or group information workspaces, group discussions, posting to team- or organisation-wide blogs, managing team projects and notifying employees about alerts.

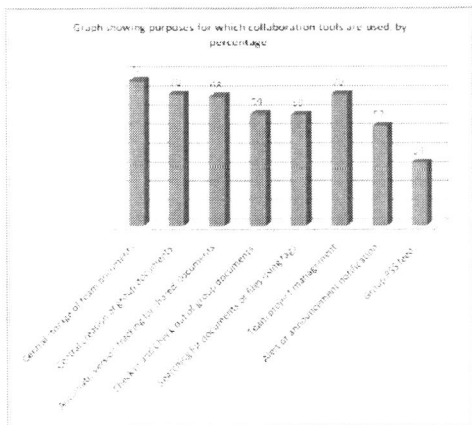

## Figure 4: The purposes for which collaboration tools are used

A survey (see Figure 4) carried out by IT Governance Ltd in May 2008 shows the purposes for which collaboration tools are used, by percentage. The table below gives details of a number of collaboration tools.

| Collaboration tool | Description |
|---|---|
| Huddle www.huddle.net | Huddle combines online collaboration, project management and document sharing using social networking principles. |
| Near-time www.near-time.net | Web-based on-demand collaboration tool. |
| Central Desktop www.centraldesktop.com | Web-based collaboration tool. |
| Nexo www.nexo.com | Free Web-based tool which enables websites and e-mail lists to be created, sharing of pictures, videos and files and online discussions. |

| | |
|---|---|
| Collanos<br>www.collanos.<br>com | Enables a single space to share, interact and collaborate with a team by sharing e-mails, messages, documents, tasks, comments and versions, etc. Downloadable tool which includes a free version as well as subscription-based features. |
| OpenTeams<br>www.openteams.<br>com | Collaboration tool which enables project management, blogging and social networking. |
| SharePoint<br>www.microsoft.<br>com/sharepoint | Microsoft Enterprise product. It doesn't contain all the features of Web 2.0 but is, nevertheless, a collaboration tool. |
| Basecamp<br>www.basecamp<br>hq.com | Web-based project management tool which supports all aspects of group project management as well as 'to-do' lists, message boards and file-sharing. |

| Skire http://www.skire. com | Offers Web-based 'capital program management', 'integrated workplace management' and 'project portfolio management'. |
|---|---|
| Open-Xchange http://www.open-xchange.com | Provider of downloadable open source e-mail and collaboration solutions. |
| Daptiv http://www.daptiv .com | On-demand leader in collaborative business software. Formerly known as eProject. |
| Backpack www.backpackit. com | Web-based tool. Enables to-do lists, announcements and group calendars to be shared online. |

**Table 2: Available collaboration tools**

**Online services**

IT is increasingly being used in the public sector to replace processes which were previously manual, and which depended on face-to-face encounters. For example, in the UK it is possible to go online to apply for a passport, renew the annual car tax and claim benefits. Some of these systems use more online features than others. For example, the HMRC child benefit website has an online enquiry service although, at present, queries to the HMRC tax credit office are only available by telephone or post.

## CHAPTER 8: OFFICE SUPPLIES AND STAFF REFRESHMENTS

Your secondary carbon footprint will include the various supplies you use in the office, the way you handle staff refreshments and, logically, how you source office furniture. Many of these issues may be tackled within a resource efficiency initiative (see Chapter 10). How far any organisation is prepared to take some of these issues will depend on their own culture, on the identifiable environmental benefits and on the cost-benefit analysis. Many organisations will take the view that their fiduciary duty to their shareholders requires them to maximise profits (in both the short and long terms); others will take the view that they should be maximising profits in a way that is environmentally responsible.

Virtually every aspect of life in the office is capable of being greened, from the type of disposable cups provided through to the janitorial supplies that are used. There are a large number of e-commerce outlets that specialise in supplies for the Green Office; a brief visit to three or four of them will reveal the range of environmentally friendly products available, and a straightforward cost-comparison will enable any organisation to decide whether or not there are products it wishes to investigate further.

A common area, and one on which many printer manufacturers have focused, is that of recycling toner and printer cartridges. Throughout the world millions of tonnes of hard, non-biodegradable plastic and loose toner powder are deposited in landfill sites from toner cartridges and inkjets which ought to be recycled. Landfill releases harmful toxins and chemicals into the land whilst also taking thousands of years to degrade; incineration pollutes the environment by discharging the toxins into the air, as well as increasing the $CO_2$ emissions as the cartridges are burnt. Printer toner cartridges contain very fine particulate powder which, although the constituents may not be toxic, can present a minor hazard; toner cartridges have been classified as hazardous waste in the EU since 2005 and arrangements must be made for them to be recycled.

The Green Office will buy remanufactured, refilled or recharged cartridges and will recycle its cartridges as they become available. There is such a big range of environmentally appropriate cartridges, and of recycling, refilling and renewal schemes available that any organisation can quickly identify one that will suit its requirements. Buy only from a reputable supplier of recycled products who can accurately specify and guarantee their quality. Ensure that the supplier guarantees that the recycled cartridge will not damage the printer and, finally, make sure that the quality of your printing meets your business requirements – both at the time of printing and later (for example, ink that fades may not be very useful).

## Catering and staff refreshments

Virtually every aspect of how you provide your staff with refreshments is capable of contributing to your carbon footprint or in some way damaging the environment. Kettles and water boilers consume energy, as do fridges, microwaves and dishwashers. It would be worth assessing the carbon footprint of facilities provided for staff, and then developing more eco-friendly alternatives. There are potential bottom-line benefits as well. For instance, a typical vending machine will use over £420-worth of electricity per year if left on for 24 hours per day. If switched off overnight and at weekends, energy could be saved and $CO_2$ emissions reduced by one tonne per year.

# CHAPTER 9: WATER USAGE

Reduction in water usage will not directly reduce the organisation's carbon footprint; for many organisations, though, a reduction in water usage is seen as contributing to an environmentally friendly work place.

The first stage in assessing water use within the workplace is to calculate how much water is being used. The best way to do this is to create what is called a site water balance.

A water balance is a numerical account of where water enters and leaves the office site, and where it is used in the meantime. Create an office water delivery chart that provides an overview of the key uses of water on the site and helps assess and control water use and effluent production. Such a water balance can help organisations reduce their water use, save money and increase profitability.

## Six-stage programme

The UK government-funded programme Envirowise[34], set up to offer businesses advice about reducing their impact on the environment, has a six-stage procedure to help organisations construct their own water balance.

1   Obtain commitment of senior management and assess the resources required.

---

[34] www.envirowise.gov.uk.

2    Collect together all appropriate data, such as water bills and meter readings. Ideally these should account for 80% of the water paid for.

3    Using a sketch diagram or flow chart, show all the areas and processes that use water. This should include the location of water meters, waste discharge points and any water wastage such as leaky pipes.

4    Quantify and record each area of water use and effluent flow in the form of units, then work out the appropriate costs.

5    Identify the areas where water savings can be achieved. Use the balance to rank target areas according to volume, potential payback periods.

6    Monitor progress of actions by conducting regular reviews and updates.

The full programme is detailed in the downloadable Envirowise guide *Tracking Water Use to Cut Costs*, which also provides a variety of free monitoring tools.

The Building Research Establishment (BRE) has set a best-practice water consumption target of 4m³ per employee per year. This is only an approximate target and would be higher for larger offices or those with catering facilities.

The formula for how much water the average employee in your office consumes in a year is:

Annual water consumption ÷ number of employees = water consumption per annum.

# CHAPTER 10: RESOURCE EFFICIENCY, WASTE AND RECYCLING

'Resource efficiency' is the term used to describe a structured environmental initiative that has the potential to save organisations a lot of money.

According to Envirowise, the UK government-funded organisation: 'waste costs money, typically up to 4% of business turnover and, by finding ways to reduce waste, your company could become more profitable'. The following guidance is from the Envirowise website and is so clear and straightforward that we have reproduced it here in its entirety.

## Waste minimisation and the waste hierarchy

To make savings in your waste costs and reduce the impact on the environment, following the waste hierarchy helps to identify different options by ranking them in order of environmental impact. Start at the top of the hierarchy to eliminate all waste where possible.

*Eliminate*

Eliminating waste entirely may not always be possible, but not creating it in the first place reduces the costs of raw materials.

*Reduce*

Reducing the amount of waste you produce can be achieved in a number of ways, including the amount of packing used, reduce off-cuts and rejects, send information electronically, purchase material in bulk and use returnable containers.

*Reuse*

To limit extra spend of buying items in, many can be reused to reduce waste.

For example:

- packaging – boxes can be reused many times
- printer toner cartridges – choose a supplier which has a returns policy so that they can be refilled and used again

- paper – reuse paper from misprints and drafts as scrap paper in the office

- drums – many raw materials are delivered in drums that can be washed and returned to the supplier, or reused on site as waste containers

- furniture and textiles – waste furniture and textiles may be of use to charities or to waste exchange groups.

*Recycle*

Recycling is an increasing requirement through legislation in order to reduce the impact on the environment. Many items can now be recycled. Speak to your local recycling centre or waste management contractor to find out what they are and how they should be segregated. Ensure that you have clearly labelled recycling bins in strategic locations throughout the office/building to make it easy for staff to recycle.

*Disposal*

Disposal is the last resort when the other hierarchy options have been exhausted. There are legal obligations that all producers and handlers of waste need to comply with, so it is important that you contact your waste management contractor to discuss options like recycling to make waste disposal more efficient and save money.

# ITG RESOURCES

IT Governance Ltd source, create and deliver products and services to meet the real-world, evolving IT governance needs of today's organisations, directors, managers and practitioners. The ITG website (www.itgovernance.co.uk) is the international one-stop-shop for corporate and IT governance information, advice, guidance, books, tools, training and consultancy.

www.itgovernance.co.uk/green-it.aspx is the ITG website that includes a comprehensive range of books, tools, project templates, resources and links for Green IT and ISO14001.

## Pocket Guides

For full details of the entire range of pocket guides, simply follow the links at www.itgovernance.co.uk/publishing.aspx.

The current range includes the following companions to this guide:

*Compliance for Green IT*
www.itgovernance.co.uk/products/2199.

*The Green Agenda: A Business Guide*
www.itgovernance.co.uk/products/2202.

*The Governance of Green IT*
www.itgovernance.co.uk/products/2106.

## Toolkits

ITG's unique range of toolkits includes *The Green IT Implementation Toolkit*, which contains all the tools and guidance that you will need in order to develop and implement an appropriate Green IT action plan for your organisation. Full details can be found at www.itgovernance.co.uk/products/2201.

## Best Practice Reports

ITG's new range of Best Practice Reports is now at www.itgovernance.co.uk/best-practice-reports.aspx. These offer you essential, pertinent, expertly researched information on an increasing number of key issues, including Green IT.

## Training and Consultancy

IT Governance also offer training and consultancy services across the entire spectrum of disciplines in the information governance arena. Details of training courses can be accessed at www.itgovernance.co.uk/training.aspx and descriptions of our consultancy services can be found at http://www.itgovernance.co.uk/consulting.aspx.

Why not contact us to see how we could help you and your organisation?

## Newsletter

IT governance is one of the hottest topics in business today, not least because it is also the fastest moving, so what better way to keep up than by subscribing to ITG's free monthly newsletter *Sentinel*? It provides monthly updates and resources across the whole spectrum of IT governance subject matter, including risk management, information security, ITIL and IT service management, project governance, compliance and so much more. Subscribe for your free copy at: www.itgovernance.co.uk/newsletter.aspx.